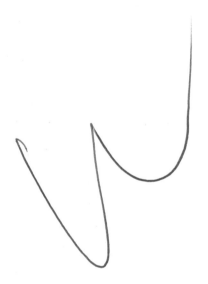

MODERN
MYTHS

MODERN
MYTHS
&
THE REALITIES BEHIND THEM

DEMETRI
MARCHESSINI

Quiller Press
London

First published 1997 by Quiller Press Limited
46 Lillie Road, London, SW6 1TN

ISBN 1 899163 30 1

Designed by Jo Lee
Printed by Biddles Ltd

Contents

Contents (continued)

Preface

The word 'essay' comes, of course, from the French word 'essais' or attempts, and that is exactly what these short pieces are - attempts to inspire the reader to think seriously about some of the real issues in modern life, and in particular those that are presently being passed over in silence or deliberately concealed. It is not expected that the reader will agree with all or even most of the views put forward by the author. It is only hoped that the reader will be incited to look at all these subjects in a new way and come to his own conclusions, rather than accept the views that are currently fashionable, and which now pass for serious thought. If the author succeeds in doing so with even a portion of his readers, he will be more than satisfied.

Chapter One

Mr Buffet

Mr Warren Buffet, the American billionaire, is well known to be opposed to leaving money to one's children. Indeed, he has been quoted as saying that leaving his money to his son would be like Jesse Owen's son receiving a 40-yard start in the 100-yard dash. The remark is interesting because it sums up in a few words many of the things that are wrong with America today.

There are, obviously, many different reasons why people leave money to their children. Clearly the strongest are the emotional ties that parents have with their children – which ties are much stronger in Europe (and especially in southern Europe) than they are in America. To many people in Europe, their children are simply extensions of themselves, like their left arm or their right leg, and in leaving money to their children, they feel that they are leaving it to themselves. Such feelings are much less common in America.

Another reason has to do with level of civilisation. In Europe, there are two kinds of people - civilised people and uncivilised people. The uncivilised people usually wish to become civilised, while the civilised people invariably wish to remain civilised - that is they want their children and grandchildren to become civilised. Now leading a civilised life has nothing to do with being rich. There are many rich people who are not civilised, and many less rich people who are very civilised. But to lead a civilised life it is necessary to have some money - not a lot of money, but a bit of money. Without any money at all, civilised life is impossible. This is another very important reason that people in Europe invariably give their children some money, in order to enable the children to live in a civilised way early on in their life, and to bring up their own children in a civilised way. This is not, however, a major preoccupation in America. Being much younger than Europe, the level of civilisation is lower, and the number of civilised people is fewer. Indeed, many of those with the opportunity to do so, do not seem to be very preoccupied with becoming civilised themselves. (Mr Buffet, for example, is not only a very intelligent man, but by all accounts, a kind and decent man. However he lives in Omaha, Nebraska, and it has been widely publicised that he spends every day of his life in his office, where he drinks countless Cherry Cokes. That is not everybody's idea of a civilised life.)

Apart from the fact that it ignores ordinary human feelings, the Jesse Owen analogy has a very significant implication - that life is simply a race for money, and that money is the only thing that counts. This is a typically

American idea, not only materialistic but also unrealistic. Intelligent, civilised people know that life is not about money. Of course, one needs some money in order to live, but life is not about money. (It is odd that many people consider inheriting money somehow unfair, yet see nothing unfair about inheriting brains, looks, abilities or virtues. And yet, all these assets are handed out just as arbitrarily as money.)

But there is a deeper and even more questionable implication to Mr Buffet's remark. What he is, in effect, suggesting is that no-one 'deserves' to have any money, unless he has made it himself. Apart from the fact that such a view has no logical foundation, it is quite repugnant if taken to its logical conclusion. Let us suppose, for example, that Mr Buffet had two sons, one of whom was decent, courageous, honest, kind and intelligent, but not particularly good at making money, while the other was greedy, mean, duplicitous, cruel and a liar, but was brilliant at making money. By Mr Buffet's criteria, the first son should be consigned to a life of restricted financial means, while the other son not only would be rich, but would 'deserve' to be rich. In short, wealth should be determined only by one's ability to make money, regardless of any other personal qualities. It is difficult to imagine a view of life that is more unprincipled, and yet at the same time, more naive - indeed very much like America today.

What Price
Principles?

One evening in 1980, when Mr Reagan was running for President and Mr Bush was running for Vice-President, Bush appeared on television for an interview. The interviewer began with a relatively sensible question, namely how could Mr Bush run on the same ticket as Mr Reagan after all the rude things that he had said about Mr Reagan in the Primary contests earlier in the year. Bush dealt with that question in the manner that was to become his hallmark - an inarticulate waffle - and ended with the promise of 'total loyalty' to Reagan. The interviewer then followed with a very weak question, which gave Mr Bush a chance to display some intelligence and some education - he asked Bush what would happen if Bush's principles ever clashed with his loyalty. Instead of taking the opportunity offered him to make a telling and effective reply, Mr Bush again resorted to inarticulate waffle.

What he should have replied, of course, was that it would be impossible for his loyalty to clash with his principles, because loyalty is one of the most important principles, and that he presumed that when the TV interviewer used the word 'principles', what he really meant were political views. It would have been interesting to see the effect on an American TV audience of the revelation that political views had nothing to do with principles - that they are merely opinions, often uninformed and always subject to change. By contrast, principles are the unchanging canons by which we try to regulate our lives - honesty, kindness, loyalty, courage, dignity, honour, etc.

The reason that this distinction has become particularly important today is that more and more people have been muddling up these two concepts, and political views have been brought more and more into people's daily lives. Some years ago I was dining with a lady who had been to a drinks party earlier in the evening, and I asked her if she had enjoyed the party. She replied that what she had enjoyed was meeting a well-known writer. After a pause, she added that she had been surprised that she had liked him so much, because his political views were so different from her own. This is of course a nonsensical statement, yet there are countless people who would have said the same. It is as nonsensical as saying that you like or dislike someone because they prefer Beethoven to Mozart or Balzac to Tolstoy. And yet this mistake is becoming almost universal, and many people now choose or reject other people not on their personal qualities, but only on the basis of their political opinions. Indeed politics have now become pervasive in almost every aspect of life.

Endless examples spring to mind: the daughter of a

friend recently graduated from the Slade (the Art College at London University). Although it was recognised within the Slade that she was one of the most talented pupils, and although she had received special prizes in both painting and drawing in her first and second years, her final grade (which was decided by a panel of 'outside experts') was the lowest in the school. The reason? - her work was described as 'reactionary' and 'bourgeois'.

In a recent article, the composer Frederick Stocken pointed out that any young composer today who dares to write melodies with harmony that people might want to listen to, is dismissed as 'irrelevant to the modern age' or as 'trying to arrest the development of music'. When he applied to study compositions at the Royal College of Music, some years ago, he was dismissed with the comment 'We do not use key signatures here'. That is equivalent to being turned down by an art college with the comment 'We do not use perspective here'.

A friend was recently putting on a series of concerts, and she received an application for tickets from a Mr & Mrs Smith. As her computer could only hold one title, she addressed the tickets to Mr Smith. She quickly received a furious letter from Mrs Smith saying she had been insulted by not being included on the envelope, and that neither she nor her husband were going to take any tickets ever again. It is easy enough to laugh, but the problem is that there are too many people today who no longer see their own ridiculousness.

A man who had worked for some years in an office, applied for a teaching position at an ex-Polytechnic (now called 'University') in the Home Counties, and gave his previous firm as a reference. The 'University' duly sent his firm a six-page typed questionnaire, which questionnaire did not ask anything either about the applicant's academic abilities or his character, but did ask for the most minute details about his political views. This is happening all over England.

More recently, the daughter of a Cabinet Minister gave interviews to the press in which she strongly criticised her father's behaviour in the House of Commons in regard to a Bill which she supported, but he did not, and she went on to suggest that he should consider resigning. Yet she had the temerity to say at the end of the interview that she hoped that this would not affect her relationship with her father in the future.

Even in the mundane world of the cinema it is difficult to find a film today that has no political orientation, and even more difficult to find a film reviewer whose review is not laced with political views.

This continued insertion into politics into our daily life is not only very distasteful – it is also extremely dangerous because it threatens the very fabric of civilisation, namely manners and principles. Without those two things, civilisation disappears and we soon move back to the jungle.

Words...

When Lenin died in 1924, his obituary in the London *Times* (at that time the most respected newspaper in the world) was headed 'Gospel of Hate'. Indeed, that is exactly what the doctrine of Socialism has always been - a gospel of hate. In those days that fact was perfectly clear to everyone. Seventy years later, however, people's perceptions and beliefs have been considerably altered, and most people no longer consider the doctrine of Socialism evil - indeed they regard those who oppose Socialism too strongly as in some ways suspect. Brian Crozier, the writer and journalist, tells the story of his first job interview in the early 1960s, when he was a young man. It was for a job on a magazine, and at a certain point, the editor said to him, 'I must make it quite clear that we are a centrist magazine' – to which Crozier replied, 'And I must make it clear that I am strongly anti-Communist.' Neither of them saw the slightest contradiction in those two statements!

How has this radical change in people's view of Socialism been effected? Obviously in many ways. Some of the best known have been: the very active propaganda machines of the Socialist/Communist countries, the continuous infiltration of the Hard Left into our educational systems, the growth of sympathy for Socialist views in the media, and the continual manipulations by the Hard Left of well-intentioned, but misguided people through their guilt feelings.

One of the most effective methods, however, has been one of the least noticed, namely the manipulation of words as a way of altering people's perception of reality. By persuading people to use words in ways that are opposite to their real meaning, the Hard Left has succeeded in making people say things that are quite different to what those people actually meant to say. From there it is only a short step to persuading people to then change their thoughts to conform to their words. To demonstrate the importance of words in our life, imagine that over the past thirty years homosexuals had been universally referred to as 'sodomites' rather than as 'gays'. Would their position and political influence in society be the same as it is today? Yet 'sodomite' is accurate, while 'gay' is an outrageous euphemism.

A good example of an influential word whose meaning has been stealthily altered is the word 'tolerant'. The dictionary definition of 'tolerant' is: 'One who tolerates opinions or practices different from his own.' The crucial phrase in that definition is 'different from his own' because it makes clear that in order to be tolerant, one must first have opinions of one's own. There is a famous occasion in history which graphically illustrates this point. When Constantinople fell in 1453, the Ottoman Turks overran Greece and the Balkans. Most people would agree that the Moslem religion is a very fervent, indeed almost a fanatical one. Yet during the almost four hundred years that the Turks occupied the Balkans, they did not interfere with the practice of the Orthodox religion in any of the Balkan countries. By contrast the Christian religion is a much more gentle religion, which preaches tolerance. Yet when the Christian Knights arrived in the Middle East with the Crusades, although many of them were very lax Christians themselves, they still chopped off the head of any infidel who refused to embrace Christianity. It was the fanatical Moslems, who were tolerant - it was the lax Christian Knights who were not.

The crucial point is that being tolerant does not mean accepting other people's views - it only means allowing others to hold views that are very different from one's own. Indeed, once the views of others have been accepted, there is no longer any need for tolerance. Yet, today, the word 'tolerant' is used in exactly the opposite way. In order to be considered 'tolerant' today, you are expected to accept the views of others, and anyone who does not do so is immediately labelled 'intolerant'.

By definition, therefore, anyone who has strong views or standards of any sort, is now automatically considered 'intolerant'. Now as traditional ideas invariably have standards imbedded in them, this results in all traditional views immediately being labelled 'intolerant'. In short, the truth has been turned inside out. It is not difficult to confuse people's minds if one goes about it systematically, and most people today - even intelligent people - are not even aware that the word 'tolerant' has been turned inside out. The truth, of course, is that it is the people who con-sider themselves 'politically correct', and who do not allow anyone to have views different from themselves, who are the intolerant ones.

George Orwell pointed out almost fifty years ago, in his famous essay 'Politics and the English Language', that there is a strong connection between politics and the debasement of language, and that slovenliness of language makes it easier to have foolish thoughts. By confusing the meaning of words, and encouraging people to use ready-made clichés, which will think their thoughts for them, political views can be transmitted into the minds of others with little difficulty. As Orwell put it, 'Ready-made clichés perform the important service of concealing your true meaning, even from yourself.'

Freedom or Democracy?

A common confusion in many people's minds is that freedom and democracy are synonymous, and that the ancient Greeks invented both. Although it might be said that the Greeks invented freedom in the sense that they were the first to establish a government without a king or tyrant, where all citizens had certain inalienable rights, democracy was quite unknown in ancient Greece. The many inhabitants of Greek cities who were not citizens had no rights at all, nor of course did the numerous slaves.

The word 'democracy' is, indeed, Greek, and it literally means 'rule of the people'. These days this has been interpreted to mean majority rule. Unfortunately, majority rule does not lend itself to freedom, because the majority invariably imposes its will (based on its own self-interest) on the minority. Freedom is the right to lead one's life as one wishes, regardless of the views of others - in other words, it is the opposite of majority rule. How is it then that freedom and democracy do sometimes co-exist?

The answer is that in most civilised countries there are Constitutions which attempt to guarantee certain individuals rights, and to protect the minority from being trampled on by the majority. The oldest and most famous of these is the American Constitution, perhaps the finest political document ever written. Most countries have Constitutions today, although most of these Constitutions are rather recent. However, many of the countries in the world that call themselves democracies - that is, countries where governments are elected by majority vote - do not have any Constitutions. In Africa, in the Arab world, in Asia, and in South America, there are countless countries that call themselves democracies, but in which the degree of freedom is very limited.

England has never been a democracy - it has always been a Constitutional Monarchy, with a House of Lords. Until recently, the English political system worked reasonably well, but its Achilles heel has always been that there was no written Constitution, and this Achilles heel has been fully exploited in the last fifty years, as much legislation has been enacted that goes violently against English traditions, and against the wishes of the English people. The English political system is such that rarely, if ever, does any political party have the majority of the country behind it. Mrs Thatcher never received more than 42% to 43% of the popular vote, while the last Labour government received only 37% or 38% of the popular vote. Yet even with a minority of the popular vote, the Government is able to impose its will on the country.

In the late 1930s, when President Roosevelt, who had

won an electoral majority, wanted to pass various legislative measures which were Socialist in nature, he was prevented from doing so by the US Supreme Court, which rejected several such laws on the grounds of unconstitutionality. If England had had a Constitution similar to the American one, much of the legislation enacted by both parties over the last fifty years would not have been possible, and some of the controversial issues that are debated today (the banning of hunting, for example) would not even be discussed, because they would be in contravention of any Constitution.

What is the solution then for England? Under the guise of 'the common good', freedoms are continually being taken away by both parties, and further freedoms are being taken away by the EU. How is one to protect one's rights in this atmosphere? This is perhaps the most important question that the younger generation must address.

If there is one thing more than any other that distinguishes a civilised country from an uncivilised one, it is the existence in that country of a 'rule of law', that is a firm legal system that is always upheld. Countries which lack such a system, have only a 'rule of man'. There are no firm laws, and decisions are arrived at only according to the personal whims or self-interest of whoever happens to be deciding the case - dictators, ministers, judges, juries etc.

It has been clear for some years now that rule of law has been slowly disappearing in America, and that it is no longer possible to predict the outcome of any case in the law courts, regardless of how clear the facts are. When a burglar who falls through a skylight and hurts himself can recover damages from the owner of the house; and when a

U.S. Supreme Court judge openly declares that he is not obliged to decide cases on the basis of the wording of the Constitution, but can 'interpret' that wording in accordance with his own political views, we are no longer under a 'rule of law'. As a result, the level of civilisation in America is being continually eroded. Regrettably, this trend has spread to England, and there have been many examples recently, in English courts, of cases that were decided neither by the wording nor by the intent of the law.

This breakdown of law is connected with another phenomenon that is just as unacceptable in a civilised country – namely, the use of force to obtain political ends or other self-interests. A recent case in England graphically illustrates both of these points. Three women broke into a British Aerospace factory at night, and did £1.5 million worth of damage to a plane, because it had been sold to Indonesia, a country which did not find political favour in their eyes. Nevertheless, the women were found not guilty of causing criminal damage by the jury, who accepted the defence that the women's action was justified 'on political grounds', ie that the plane might be used in a way that they did not agree with. Now once political views are accepted as a valid defence for committing a crime, the rule of law disintegrates – everyone has different political views, and there is no crime (not even murder) which can not be justified by someone's political views. Rule of law is then soon replaced by the law of the jungle. (An interesting question to ask oneself is whether three ordinary middle-class women forty years ago would have been concerned with events taking place ten thousand miles away and entirely unconnected with their own lives, let alone would have dreamt of breaking into a factory at night and destroying expensive property.)

It is important to understand that many so-called 'peaceful' demonstrations are not peaceful at all. If 50,000 people want to assemble in Trafalgar Square, that may well be a peaceful demonstration. But if a stranger walks into your house, sits on your sofa, and refuses to move until you do something that he wants you to do, this is not at all 'peaceful'. The fact that he has not used force to come in does not make it 'peaceful', because he can be evicted only by force. He is 'peaceful' only as long as you do what he wants. The crucial point about these demonstrators is that the 'justness' or unjustness of their cause is entirely irrelevant. We all have causes that we think are just, but the mark of a civilised country is that no one except the government can ever be allowed to use force. The moment anyone else is allowed to do so, civilisation begins to fall away. Unless serious efforts are made to arrest these trends, we will soon follow America on the road to barbarism.

Is Marriage Dead?

This is a question that one hears frequently these days. To answer it, one must first have a clear idea of what marriage means, and the basic problem is that most people today no longer do have any idea of what marriage means. Marriage is, above all, a promise - a promise made before God, and in the presence of the world, that one will look after another person for the rest of one's life. If one fails to do so, then one has broken one's sacred word. If this were kept in mind, many marriage problems would recede.

I am not, of course, suggesting that there should be no divorce. On the contrary, human nature is weak and imperfect, and there has been divorce in the Christian religion since the 4th century. (Some Christian churches have most unwisely abolished it, and have since regretted doing so.) But the grounds acceptable for divorce must be serious ones: mental instability, drug addiction, alcoholism, homosexuality, criminal acts, violent behaviour, non-consummation of the marriage, etc. What is not a serious reason is that one party wants to sleep with someone else. If marriage is not for life, it has no meaning, and if it is to remain the most important institution of our society, there must be penalties for those who break their vows for frivolous reasons.

That is why divorce can never be 'no-fault', as some people today pretend it should be, because the two important issues in every divorce - children and money - can then never be decided equitably. 'No-fault' divorce has a doubly bad effect - it discourages people who wish to behave properly from getting married, while it encourages those who wish to behave badly to do so because they know that they will not be punished. If a wife chooses to bolt, why should her husband lose his children, and his money as well? If a husband decides to go off with another woman, why should the wife's life become poorer and disagreeable as a result? There is always 'fault' in any divorce, but 'fault' does not mean counting up all the unkind things each person has said or done during the marriage. 'Fault' simply means that whichever partner wishes to break up the marriage is the one who must take the consequences. Alternatively, if one party has serious grounds for divorce, then it is the other party who must bear the consequences.

But for the marriage to survive, it is not sufficient simply to prevent it from being terminated frivolously - it is also necessary to create conditions for happiness and contentment. It has been made clear time and time again that the single most important requirement for a successful marriage is that both people must love each other. This may seem obvious, and yet many people today do not seem to be aware of it. By loving, I mean a strong affection, something which lasts for life - not just 'being in love'. Being 'in love' is very nice, but unfortunately it rarely lasts very long. The worst reason of all to get married is sex, and yet this seems to be the most usual reason at the moment in the Anglo-Saxon world. Of course, once the sexual attraction is gone, there is nothing left, and the game of musical chairs begins.

Before deciding to marry, a man should first ask himself some of the following questions: 'Is this the woman with whom I want to have children? Is this the woman by whom I would like my children brought up? Will I be proud of her when she walks into a room in ten years' time? In twenty years' time? Do I find her presence charming and attractive? Do I enjoy spending time alone with her? Do we have the same values? Is there a crunch (and *there will always be a crunch*) will I be able to rely on her loyalty? A woman should ask herself similar questions.

Unfortunately, very few people are able to work all these things out when they are young, particularly if they have never been told about them. Young people must rely on their instinct, because as yet they do not have enough experience to formulate and articulate these thoughts. If their instincts are good, they may be successful. But instincts are influenced very much by upbringing and education. Two generations ago, both upbringing and education were conducive to marriage. Today, the opposite is true, and everything that the younger generation hears is inimical to marriage.

A further threat to marriage today is 'feminism'. Not old-fashioned 'feminism' which simply demanded equal treatment for women, but modern 'feminism' which posits that all women *must* work, that their children should be looked after *by others*, that the traditional protection that men give to women should be discarded in favour of 'independence', that women should be continually competing with men and be at war with them, etc. It is interesting that very few young men attack feminism, and it is easy to see why – 'feminism' allows them to do anything they like with a girl without the slightest responsibility. In short 'feminism' suits men right down to the ground. It is women whom it does not suit. Clever women have always understood this, but the less clever and unrealistic ones have not.

If the present trends persist, marriage will disappear in the Western World, at least in its present form. What many people seen to forget is that monogamous marriage only exists in the Western World, and that in the greater part of the world there was and is no Western-style marriage. Men simply have women – some are called wives (usually several), some are concubines, some are just mistresses. How many women a man has depends only on how rich he is. Even if a man can afford only one wife, the wife is usually treated like a slave. Some years ago I visited an Indian acquaintance whose wife came from the richest and most powerful family in India. Yet she was not allowed ever to turn her back on her husband, and whenever she left the room that he was in, she would go out of the door backwards.

It is only in the Western World that monogamous marriage has flourished. There have been several reasons for this, but unfortunately all of them are crumbling at the moment. The first, and perhaps most important, was the fact that the Christian church (and the Jewish faith) preached monogamy. This was unprecedented at the time

– until then polygamy had been usual. Unfortunately, religious belief today is on the wane, and with it the religious underpinning for marriage. Another reason that marriage has flourished in the West is that only in the Western World was there any differentiation between women – some were considered ladies, and some were not. This differentiation was not instigated by men (as feminists would have us believe) – the vast majority of men would be perfectly content if all women were tarts, and they could just float from one to another without the slightest responsibility. On the contrary, the differentiation was done by *women,* by the women who wished to raise themselves above the level of 'women' to the level of 'ladies' and 'wives', and in so doing to gain men's respect, and men's protection. Again this differentiation is becoming blurred today. With the 'emancipation' of women, more and more women think that they must behave like men, and it is becoming more difficult to find 'ladies' in the traditional sense. A third reason is that the higher standard of living in the Western World over the last eight hundred years has enabled women to create relatively comfortable homes for their husbands – refuges from the jungle of the outside world. This has been a strong attraction for men to marry, but this, too, is now under attack, as many women have become more interested in their own careers than in creating a home or looking after their family. Thus the incentives for men to marry are rapidly disappearing.

One can already see the beginnings of marriage disintegration in the young people. The young men don't marry the girls any more - they live with them for a few years - and then discard them. In the meantime, the girls lose their youth, their morale, and sometimes their looks. Even the older generation of men, who have been married for many years, now have no compunction in abandoning their wives in middle age, and leaving them to fend for themselves. (Imagine if a young man today were to ask a young girl to marry him, but were to warn her at the same time that in twenty years when their children were grown up and she had lost her looks, he would leave her for a young women. What kind of reply would that young man receive? A good slap around the face? And yet that is exactly what many men are doing today without being penalised in any way.)

These trends can be reversed only when it is clearly understood by women that men are not obliged to marry them, and that on the one hand they must therefore make the prospect of marriage attractive to men, and on the other hand, must desist from accepting the role of concubines and living with young men outside of marriage.

Feeling Guilty?

I have a friend, who comes from an old upper class American family. She was brought up with traditional values, but without ostentation, and her parents sent her to schools where she received a good education. When her own daughter recently reached school age, she was sent to the same girls' school which her mother had attended, and which is still considered the best girls' school in that city.

She was, therefore, horrified to find out that the school today bore no resemblance to the school which she had attended twenty-five years before. Like almost all educational institutions in America today, the school had accepted many students who were not academically qualified, solely for political reasons. Naturally, in order to ensure that all these unqualified students then were able to graduate, it was necessary that the academic standards of the school be drastically lowered. As a result, the education that the school now offers bears no resemblance to any traditional education. Furthermore, the girls are not allowed to play any competitive sports or games, 'because someone would lose' (in the world of the Left, no-one is ever allowed to lose). One day my friend rang the teacher to apologise because her daughter had been ill and had not been able to finish her homework for that day. She was startled to hear the teacher reply, 'Don't worry - your daughter is the only one in the class who ever does any homework, anyway.' And this is the best girls' school in the city.

Now, there is nothing particularly unique about this situation - the same thing is happening all over America. But there is one interesting aspect of the case, which is that the headmistress of this school is my friend's first cousin, and had come from exactly the same background as she had. When I asked my friend why her cousin had thrown up all the values that she had been brought up with, and fallen for such left-wing nonsense, she replied, 'Guilt - she is riddled with guilt.'

Recently one of our most senior diplomats published his memoirs, in which memoirs he discourses at a certain point on Ronald Reagan, and suggests that Reagan resembled Mrs. Thatcher in that both of them had worked their way up in the world by themselves, and had 'no guilt feelings' about others. Further on in the same passage, the diplomat again notes with surprise that both Reagan and Mrs. Thatcher strongly felt that 'the more fortunate should not have any sense of guilt about the less fortunate'. In other words, our diplomat is suggesting that guilt feelings are normal, and that there was something very

25

odd about Mr. Reagan and Mrs. Thatcher for not having them. Now the diplomat saying these things was not only distinguished, and intelligent, but most importantly was also a Conservative. Now even distinguished Conservatives accept the Hard Left Thesis of universal guilt, it is difficult to see who there remains to resist it.

To any rational person, the suggestion that one should feel guilt about people whom one has never met, or things that one has no connection with is laughable. But more than that, it is also extremely pernicious because of all the methods employed by the Hard Left to achieve their aims, guilt has been the most effective.

Of course, it goes without saying that the myths that are propagated to promote this sense of guilt are invariably completely untrue. One of the most ingrained is the widespread belief that the black slaves who were brought to the New World in the 17th and 18th centuries had been enslaved by white men, and that all of us today are therefore somehow 'responsible' for this crime, and for the welfare of all of their descendants. If one did not know better, one would get the impression from those who propagate this myth that this was the only known instance of slavery in the history of the world. The truth is that slavery has existed all over the world for thousands of years, and that it was neither particularly American, nor particularly white. Until comparatively recently in history slavery was not even controversial in most parts of the world because outside of the West the concept of freedom simply did not exist. As the American scholar, Orlando Paterson, wrote: 'There was no word for the word 'freedom' in most non-Western languages before contact with Western peoples.'

More importantly, slavery had existed extensively throughout Central and West Africa long before white men appeared there. Three powerful African kingdoms, Ghana, Songhay and Mali, all relied on slave labour. Nor were their slaves exclusively blacks - Arab slaves were purchased from the East, while any white Europeans who were unfortunate enough to be shipwrecked were also enslaved. During the height of the American slave trade, almost three-quarters of the population of black Africans were already slaves. It does not require a great deal of intelligence to understand that when European slave ships came to West Africa, the captains did not send their sailors running around the country with lassoes, looking for slaves. They simply bought as many slaves as they needed from the black slave traders of West Africa.

In short, the notion that Europe imposed the slave trade on Africa is without any foundation in history, and the truth is that all the blacks who were sold into slavery in the New World were sold by other blacks. This truth was stated by Zora Neale Hurston, the black feminist writer in the early part of this century, who said '…the inescapable fact that stuck in my craw was: my people had sold me…'

The greatest irony (and the greatest hypocrisy) regarding slavery come from the fact that, although it existed universally and was not confined to the West, it was the West that abolished it. Indeed, the first serious challenge to the institution of slavery was the United States Declaration of Independence. As Tocqueville wrote: 'We have seen something absolutely without precedent in history - servitude abolished, not by the desperate effort of the slave but by the enlightened will of the master…' Yet very few scholars discuss or even mention this point.

In 1772 Britain was the first country in the world to abolish slavery on its soil, and by 1833 slavery had been abolished throughout the British Empire. The movement then spread to France, which forbade slavery in its territories in 1848, and later to other European nations. The African reaction to this abolition could have been the inspiration of a film comedy (perhaps written by Evelyn Waugh, and starring Peter Sellers). Tribal leaders from Gambia, the Congo, Dahomey and other nations that had prospered under slavery, sent delegations to London and Paris to vigorously protest at its abolition.

Surprisingly, the practice of slavery has persisted into the 20th century in many parts of Africa, the Middle East, and the Far East. Indeed Saudi Arabia and the Yemen did not outlaw slavery until 1962. British Anti-Slavery International, which tries to monitor the practice of slavery in the world today, estimates that in Mauritania alone almost 100,000 people are enslaved today.

And yet this myth of black enslavement by whites is not only widely disseminated, but is accepted as gospel. Very few people have made any effort to ascertain the true facts, and countless numbers continue to be racked by 'guilt'. Yet Zora Hurston wrote: '…Slavery is the price I paid for civilisation, and that is worth all that I have paid through my ancestors…'

Morality, Legality and Homosexuality

A distinction that is often confused in many people's minds today is the distinction between morality and legality. Morals are, of course, the unchanging principles by which we try to live our lives. Laws, on the other hand, are merely decisions made by those in power, often for their own political convenience, and often later altered. Although the two concepts sometimes overlap in that some laws are in accord with morality, quite often law and morality have nothing to do with each other. For example, if one parks one's car on a double yellow line, it is clearly illegal, but it is certainly not immoral. Similarly, if one betrays one's greatest friend in his hour of need, it is despicably immoral, but it is not illegal.

The purpose of any sensible law should be to create a condition which is necessary for the common good - for example the maintenance of law and order so that people can live without fear, or the creation of roads and railroads so that travel and commerce are facilitated. It is not the prerogative of government (at least in free countries) to decide and impose their morality on their citizens. Almost everyone would agree that murder is immoral, but the real reason that it must be illegal is that if people were allowed to go around killing other people with impunity, society would disintegrate and we would be back in the jungle. Similarly, if people were allowed to rob banks, very soon there would not be any banks, which is why bank robbery must be illegal - not only because it is immoral, but because it is intolerable. Whenever any government has tried to impose, purely for 'moral' reasons, a law which is unnecessary to the common good, the results have invariably been disastrous. Perhaps the best known example of this kind was Prohibition in America in the 1920ís, which not only was a complete fiasco, but which spawned organised crime, corrupted the police (no one is keen to enforce a law that they do not believe in), and established generally hypocrisy, all of which remain an endemic part of America today.

The above distinction is crucial in understanding the present problems relating to homosexuality. Until recently homosexuality was a criminal offence, and offenders went to jail. When various countries, including England, decided that it was not civilised to put people in jail for their sexual practices, and abolished homosexuality as a crime, most civilised people applauded this step. Certainly there have been many homosexuals in history who have enormously enriched the world. Certainly, the world would have been a much poorer place if Leonardo and Michelangelo had spent their lives in jail.

But at the same time it must be remembered that homosexuality is, and has been, a major sin in the Christian religion (and indeed in most other religions) for several thousand years, and that the vast majority of people continue to find it repugnant. It is important to understand that none of these things change simply because the government has passed a law. In other words, homosexuality may be no longer illegal, but it continues to be immoral to the vast majority of the world. Of course, very few of us envisaged what was going to take place once homosexuality became legal, in particular the way it was to become politicised. Because this is the real problem. Homosexuality has become one of the main causes of the Hard Left, and of all those who wish to destroy religious beliefs and traditional family relationships. This is what is really behind the homosexual demonstrations, the continual publicity, and the clamouring for 'homosexual rights'. (Of course it is perfectly clear that there is no such thing as 'homosexual rights', because homosexuals have no more rights than anyone else.) It is precisely these attempts to gain special concessions which cause many of the problems associated with homosexuality.

The fact is that no-one (or practically no-one) cares what homosexuals do, as long as they keep it to themselves. We all have homosexual friends - we do not tell them about our sex lives; they do not tell us about theirs. That is the way civilised people behave. What is unacceptable is the flaunting of homosexuality.

Even more intolerable is the implanting of homosexuality into the school system. Young children in State schools are given picture books showing two men in bed with a child standing nearby, and are told that this is a 'family group'. Small children are being instructed about

AIDS; students are not allowed to see Shakespeare's Romeo and Juliet because it is too 'heterosexual', etc. The idea is to persuade our children and grandchildren that homosexuality is perfectly acceptable behaviour.

All the problems connected with homosexuality would recede if the distinction between morality and legality were kept clearly in mind, and if it were understood that normal people are just as free to consider homosexuality immoral and unacceptable, as homosexuals are free to continue practising it.

What is Religion anyway?

As religion is no longer fashionable, it is not surprising that people are losing sight of what it means. Whether one is religious or not religious does not in any way depend on how well or how badly one behaves in life. Indeed the whole point of religion is to help people who are behaving badly to behave better, and to come closer to God. If everyone always lived up to their religion, there would no longer be any need for religion. It is precisely for those who sin that religion is necessary. Whether one is religious or not depends on one thing, and one thing only - does one believe? There are many atheists in the world who are very fine people. But they are not Christians because they do not believe. There are also many Christians who are not always nice people, but this does not change the fact that as long as they continue to believe, they are

Christians. To be a Christian simply means that one believes in the teachings of Christ. If one does not believe in Christ's teachings, that does not necessarily mean one is not religious (there are many other religions), but it does mean that one is not a Christian.

Now the Church of England has always been considered a respectable religion. Unfortunately, however, I would suggest that it no longer accepts the teachings of Christ. I am referring, in particular, to the questions of homosexuality and the ordination of women. Taking homosexuality first, it is undeniable that homosexuality has been considered to be one of the major sins in the Christian religion for two thousand years (and in the Old Testament long before that). The enormity of this sin has been made abundantly clear in both Testaments. How is it possible suddenly to pretend that it is no longer a sin, and that homosexuality has suddenly become acceptable behaviour?

The issue of women priests is quite a different one, in that no-one has ever suggested that there is anything immoral about women being priests. Indeed, before Christ the priests in pagan religions were often women. The point is that Christ obviously did not want women priests, and that it was one of many changes that he made from the pagan past. Some supporters of women priests try to argue that because Christ never specifically prohibited women priests, He was not really opposed to them. Are they suggesting that Christ was absent-minded? Or that He was perhaps too incompetent to arrange things as He wanted them? Or are they perhaps suggesting that eighty generations of Christian bishops have been too stupid to grasp Christ's teachings and that only the present Anglican bishops are clever enough to really understand what Christ wanted?

Such arrogance would indeed be breathtaking if their decisions had been made on religious grounds. But the truth is that they have been made on political, and only on political, grounds. Unfortunately politics is more powerful than religion in the Church of England today. Which is precisely why the Anglican Church can no longer be regarded as a serious Christian church, and is also why both its clergy and its members are leaving it in droves.

Perhaps the potentially most significant and least understood development in the religious world today is the 'ecumenical' movement - that is the desire to bring all Christian religions closer together by papering over the differences in the religious beliefs that now separate them. This idea of bringing Christians closer is superficially attractive, and there are many people - both clerics and laymen - who support the 'ecumenical' movement in good faith and with the best intentions. That is why it is important to understand that the movement is in reality a dangerous one, because at heart it is anti-religious.

The truth is that bringing different religions 'closer' can only be done by the watering down and compromising of religious beliefs. This in turn leads to diminishing their importance. Once it is accepted that actual religious beliefs are of little importance, it is only a short step to accepting that one's religion itself is of little importance. After all, what is any religion but a set of beliefs? If one religion is as good as another, and they are all interchangeable, all religions lose importance and value.

One is then left with only amorphous beliefs - some vague and woolly ideas about 'good-will towards all men', which woolly ideas can then be easily manipulated in whatever direction is politically required. That is why

there are also many people promoting the 'ecumenical'
movement who have neither good faith nor good intentions.

Chapter Two

Just what is Socialism?

As several of these essays deal with the effect of Socialism on modern life, it is important to know exactly what the words 'Socialism' and 'Socialists' mean. The dictionary defines Socialism as a policy of social organisation which advocates the redistribution of wealth, together with the ownership by the State of all means of production, of capital and of land. This is a reasonably accurate description as far as it goes, but there is a further level of meaning which one must reach in order to understand what Socialism really means. As Socialism runs strongly counter to human nature, and no-one (apart from very small groups) has ever accepted pure socialism voluntarily, in order to exist it must be imposed by coercion. Such coercion can consist of brute force, as was the case behind the Iron Curtain and is still the case in China, or it can take a more subtle but perhaps even more sinister form - the ruthless undermining of traditional institutions by the very people to whom they have been entrusted, combined with a persistent and continuous public attack on all traditional values and ideas. This is of course what has been taking place throughout the Western World, and particularly in the Anglo-Saxon world, over the last 30 years. The means used to accomplish this, although falling short of the use of actual force, are completely ruthless. They include threats, intimidation, the smearing of reputations, the ostracising of all opponents, violent demonstrations and, above all, a torrent of continuous 'disinformation' (commonly known as lies). I would suggest that only those who approve and take part in these activities are Hard Socialists (although they often call themselves by many other names). Those who take the first step, but have no stomach for the second, are only Soft Socialists.

Now it is very important to understand that the Labour Party is not Socialist, despite the famous Clause 4, because the majority of the people who vote Labour are actually more conservative than many of those in Westminster who masquerade as Conservative MPs. If they vote Labour, they do so only because they expect to benefit materially thereby. Anyone who has any doubts about that has only to have a conversation with a lorry driver or a docker for a few minutes. Furthermore, many of the leaders of the Labour Party are not Hard Socialists - most of them are Soft, and some are not Socialist at all. Imbedded within the Labour Party, however, there is a strong core of Hard Socialists - it is they who control the Party behind the scenes, and it is they who use the Party as the operating vehicle with which to achieve the society that they desire.

The question arises, if the Hard Socialists are not a majority within the Labour Party, how have they gained such effective control over the Party's machinery? The reasons are not so difficult to see - firstly, they are much better organised and more efficient than any other group in the party; secondly they are absolutely ruthless in attacking and smearing anyone who opposes them; but the most important reason is perhaps another one. If one pays lip service to goals that cannot be attained without coercion, it is then very difficult to oppose those who are prepared to implement that coercion to attain those goals. Inherent in Socialism is the belief that 'the end justifies the means'. As Lenin said, "...morality is entirely subordinated to the interests of the class struggle..." and therefore scruples and principles are irrelevant in the fight to attain their goals. That is why Soft Socialists can never stand up to the Hard ones.

Lies...

One of the most effective tools in the armour of the Hard Left has been used of propaganda words. Propaganda words are words that have no actual meaning (i.e. they have never existed in any dictionary), and are invented with the sole purpose of leaving a particular impression in the mind of the hearer. These words often end in 'ist' or 'ism'. As they have no precise meaning, once these words have been accepted into people's vocabularies, they can later be manipulated to mean whatever anyone wishes them to mean.

One of the most successful propaganda words has been the word 'capitalism'. The intention of this word is to establish the impression that the Western World lives under some sort of 'system', and that this system is based on capital. The implication, of course, is that the Western

World is materialistic and greedy. As usual with propaganda words, the truth is exactly the opposite. We in the West do not live under any 'system' at all - if our way of life is based on anything, it is based on freedom - while it is the Socialists who deny all spiritual values and pretend that happiness can be achieved simply by the redistribution of wealth. What could be more materialistic than that? But as they cannot afford to admit that they live in slavery, while we live in freedom, they use the word 'capitalism' to obscure the truth.

What is surprising, is how well they have succeeded in doing so, and to what extent the word 'capitalism' has been swallowed by and accepted in the free world. Everyone now uses it, despite the fact that it is both false and pejorative. It is as if you or I had been called an insulting name, and had then not only accepted the insult, but had even adopted the word to describe ourselves. Such idiocy is difficult to believe.

The words 'Communist' and Socialist' are themselves quite instructive. Lenin, Trotsky and Stalin were simply Socialists, and indeed the term 'Bolsheviks' refers to the way that they took control (by devious means) of the Russian Socialist party. They were simply the first Socialists who were prepared to shed blood to achieve their goals. Because this blood later became unacceptable to the rest of the world, Russian Socialists were termed 'Communists', as if to differentiate them in some way from other Socialists. The truth was that as far as their aims were concerned, there was not the slightest difference between them and other Socialists. The only difference was the level of violence that they were prepared to use to achieve those goals.

A more recent propaganda word is 'homophobe'. I

was rather surprised when I heard an American friend use it recently, because she is both intelligent and educated. I pointed out to her that there is no such word as 'homophobe' in any dictionary. She admitted that she had had some doubts about the word because the first half of the word has a Latin root, while the second half has a Greek root, which is a nonsense, and also because even if the two halves of the word were compatible, the literal meaning would be 'someone who is afraid of men', which is not at all the way the word is used. I hope that my American friend has now given up using the word 'homophobe', but as long as other intelligent and educated people continue to do so, the Hard Left will be achieving its purpose.

Yet another phrase that is used to manipulate opinion is the phrase 'Right Wing'. Originally the Socialists were termed 'the Left', because they sat on the left side of the Chambre des Deputes in Paris. As long as all non-Socialists were united in their opposition to Socialism, it did not matter so much if the Socialists were called 'the Left', and the non-Socialists 'the Right'. But as the trend towards Socialism has gathered pace, and more and more people have gone at least part of the way towards 'Socialism', there has now developed an enormous political spectrum with a vast amorphous 'centre', so that those who continue to oppose Socialism - 'the Right' - are now at the edge of the spectrum, instead of being in the middle of it, and are now considered 'extreme'.

The so-called 'centre' is composed of people who may not entirely agree with Socialism, but who have accepted some Socialist ideas, and in any case are not prepared to oppose Socialism - they are rather like someone who thinks they can peacefully share a cage with a tiger, a category that now includes many Conservative MPs.

43

Anyone who continues to be anti-Socialist, as Mr Crozier was thirty-five years ago, is today labelled 'Right Wing'. As 'Right Wing' is also the label given to supporters of dictatorships, the implication is that the more strongly one opposes Socialism, the more one is in favour of some sort of dictatorship. As usual, exactly the opposite is true - it is precisely because Socialism is a dictatorship (and indeed the most vicious kind of dictatorship), that those who cherish freedom oppose it.

In short, we have now reached the point where it is no longer acceptable to attack Socialism. One is allowed to disagree with some or all of their policies, one can say that 'it does not work', but one can no longer attack the spirit of Socialism; one can no longer denounce it as a malicious and dishonest creed, based on envy and hate, which appeals to all of man's worst instincts; one can certainly no longer call it a 'Gospel of Hate'. Furthermore, as the 'Hard Left' goes continuously further and further to the 'left' (which means against all traditional values), it pulls the so-called 'centre' with it. The 'centre' has become a kind of airport escalator, moving continuously to the left.

Propaganda words have another use which is extremely important. They are the means used to discredit anyone who dares to attack Hard Left policies. As it is impossible for the Hard Left to make any rational response to criticism, they invariably have to resort to personal abuse - attacks 'ad hominem' - in order to try to discredit their opponents. Thus, anyone who criticises what is going on in education is immediately labelled 'elitist'; anyone who criticises the feminist movement is 'sexist' or 'chauvinist'; anyone who criticises the homosexual movement is a 'homophobe', etc. Once someone has been so labelled (and thus discredited), he is no longer worthy of being given a serious reply, and what he says can then safely be ignored. Thus the Hard Left can avoid having to make any serious reply to their critics. As for their own followers and sympathisers, those minds are already closed - they are rather like a passionate religious sect, who consider that there is no point in talking to anyone who does not share their religion.

Perhaps the most famous Socialist propaganda technique is the technique known as 'The Big Lie'. First popularised by Marx, and later brought to an art by the Russians, it consists of simply continuing to repeat something that one knows is quite untrue - until it is finally accepted as truth, (if not by everyone, at least by many). One might consider this a somewhat babyish technique, and yet it has often proved extremely effective. Unfortunately human nature is both weak and foolish, and if people hear something often enough, many begin to believe it. What makes the Hard Left so dangerous is that they have grasped the essence of human weakness, and that they attack precisely at the places where human nature is most vulnerable.

...and Truth

Some years ago a young lady sitting next to me at dinner expressed the view that it was impossible for anyone to be objective, because one's views are entirely shaped by one's background and environment. What she was suggesting, of course (perhaps unintentionally), was that reason and logic do not exist. I was rather surprised to hear such childish views from someone who had recently received a good degree from Oxford, but as I later learned it was naive of me to be surprised, because such views have been circulating at every university in England for many years. At one time such views were known as 'Relativism' and were fashionable in intellectual circles. Although they are now no longer in fashion in the highest intellectual circles, they continue to be widely taught at lower levels, and they are now embedded in the minds of many people. When I pointed out to the young lady in question that the view she had just expressed was simply standard Socialist dogma, without any intellectual merit, she replied: 'But, surely, all intelligent people think this way.' In short, she was even more surprised that I was rejecting her theory, than I had been to hear her put it forward.

It is quite obvious why the Hard Left insist that no one can be objective - objectivity is the one thing that they cannot pretend to have. No matter what other qualities they can aspire to, it is patently obvious even to their sympathisers that they are not remotely objective. Now if the rest of the world is allowed to be objective, when they are clearly not objective, the Hard Left would quickly become ridiculous. The only way they can evade this problem is by trying to pretend that no-one can be objective. This puts them on the same footing as everyone else, and therefore able to reject all criticism by alleging that their critics are not 'objective'.

A thesis very similar to the 'impossibility of objectivity', is the old cliché that there is no such thing as truth, and that everything is 'relative'. This theory is a favourite of Socialists in every sphere, but particularly in education, where they often claim that there is no truth in history (that is at least until the history books have been altered to suit Socialist convenience). One of the problems encountered in Eastern Europe after the fall of the Iron Curtain was that all the history books in schools had to be completely re-written, because under Socialist rule they had been altered beyond recognition, and no longer bore the slightest connection to facts or reality. (In England, the Socialists have succeeded in accomplishing the same thing, but without the need of an Iron Curtain. Despite seventeen years of Conservative rule, we are still waiting for the re-writing.)

One of the professors at my university was fond of saying, 'Whenever anyone tells you that there is no truth, it usually means that he is about to tell you a very big lie.' I have invariably found that advice to be accurate. It is difficult to believe that intelligent people can still be taken in by such childish assertions, and yet they still continue to be. Socialist tactics invariably remain the same - facts and reason must be discredited, lies and fantasies must prevail. And in our educational system, both state and private, they certainly do.

"Equality of Opportunity"

When the Socialists took control of our educational system thirty or so years ago, and began systematically to destroy traditional education, the slogan that they used to justify their actions was 'equality of opportunity'. Of course, everyone knows that there can be no such thing as equality of opportunity in life, because life is not a race for an established prize - everyone has different aspirations and different abilities. Nevertheless, it was a persuasive slogan to those who did not think too deeply about it, and the majority acquiesced, or at least did not raise any objections to the rape of traditional education, and the lowering of academic standards.

Today the true colours of the Hard Left, and the naiveté of the majority have been made clear, because the Hard Left is no longer talking about 'equality of opportunity', but rather of 'equality of attainment'. In other words, regardless of how intelligent or unintelligent students are, regardless of what talents they have, and regardless of how hard they have worked, everyone must receive the same grades, must be considered equal scholastically, and must have access to the same jobs. Under no circumstances is anyone allowed to be shown to be scholastically inferior to others.

In order to maintain this fiction, the one thing that must be avoided at all costs are tests, because tests give objective results. That is why the teachers' unions in England (who, of course, are controlled by the Hard Left) have been resisting any kind of testing so strongly. Although only roughly 20 per cent of the teachers are members of the unions, nevertheless the union's influence is strong. At the moment, in the State school system, grades are determined only by 'coursework' (i.e. student papers, on which it is easy for students to have outside help - or in other words, to cheat) and by 'teacher assessment' of classwork, which is, of course, purely subjective opinion. Indeed it was recently reported in the press that a suggestion in a State school to give the students homework was firmly turned down by the authorities of the school. The explanation given was, 'Everyone might not be able to do it.' Under such conditions, there is no such thing as real education - there is only fantasy.

Chapter Three

The Position of Women

The main problem in women's lives is not that they are inferior to men - they are neither inferior nor superior. Their problem is rather that nature has put them into an inferior position in life. This inferior position is a result, firstly and most importantly, of the fact that women want and need children, and that the vast majority of women are not fulfilled unless they have them. This is obviously indispensable for life - if women stopped wanting children, the human race would soon come to a stop. Women are made - physically, emotionally, mentally and in every other way - to want and to have children.

In order to have the children, however, they must first have a husband. This is not only for financial reasons, but even more for emotional security, for protection in life, and because children need a father. Furthermore, because their child-bearing age is limited, they must find husbands relatively quickly. From a physical point of view, it is best for a woman to have children in her twenties. Of course, she can still have them in her thirties, but the middle thirties is the latest realistic time that a woman can be married if she is to have children.

By contrast, men do not have to marry at all. Of course, most men also want children, but they do not have the same need for them that women have, and it is also much easier for them to have children outside of marriage. Most importantly, men have no time limits. They can marry at any age, and can have children at any age – Charlie Chaplin fathered a child in his middle eighties.

Furthermore, although marriage means security for women, it means sacrifices for men. Firstly, they have to give up their independence (which is much more important to them than women's independence is to women - women being more interested in emotional security than in independence). Secondly, marriage requires a considerable financial sacrifice for a man. A man on his own can live reasonably well on a modest income, but a family requires very substantial expenses. The reality then is - although few people are prepared to admit it - that women must persuade men (in the nicest possible way) to marry, and that unless the terms of marriage are made attractive to men, men will simply not marry.

Another disadvantage that women have is that they lose their looks much sooner than men do. Of course there are always exceptions, but once child-bearing age is past, most women quickly become much less attractive. This is extremely unfair, but it is an inescapable fact (perhaps nature has a reason for it). In any case, it means that middle-aged women no longer have much in the way of weapons, and must rely on their husbands for their security. That is why it has always been considered monstrous for a man to leave his wife in middle age, when she no longer has either looks or money (there is never enough money after a divorce). He has taken the 'best years of her life', and then rejected what was left. Unfortunately, that is exactly what is happening today, because women are trying to pretend that they are 'equal' and just as 'independent', and men are using that as a pretext to discard them.

The other great disadvantage that women have is that men have all the money. This has been true from the earliest times. Women have always had to be occupied with the home and their children, and it is the men who have always gone out and supported the family. Indeed, until this century it could not have been otherwise. Today, although many women now work, men continue to be more aggressive, more ambitious, and more focused on making money. Of course there are many women in the professional and business classes who have good jobs and earn high salaries, but how many women have made enormous fortunes starting from nothing?

In short, men and women are dealing with each other from very different footings. Clever women understand that, and make the best of it (which is usually very good indeed). Women who are less clever (or less in touch with reality), try to pretend that they are on the same footing with men, invariably with disastrous results.

Feminism - old and new

'Feminism' is a term that is used very often these days, and although the idea is a very old one, it seems to hold today very different meanings for different people. There is a lady in London, whose husband is not only very rich, but also grants her every whim and spoils her in every way - yet she considers herself an ardent feminist. There is another lady in New York who, after her divorce some years ago, lived in a modest apartment with her children, and had to work in order to make ends meet. She met a rich man and eventually moved in with him together with her children. They now live together in comfort, and he happily gives her anything she wants. She has stopped working now because she finds the work disagreeable, and feels that she does not make enough money from it. She, too, considers herself an ardent feminist.

The feminists of the past fought to obtain equality of opportunity for women - in politics, in the professions, in marriage laws, in property rights and in other normal spheres of daily life. Very few people today would disagree with those aims. The new generation of feminists, however, particularly the American ones, demand 'parity', not equality (half of all positions must be held by women regardless of qualifications or availability); and their leaders and 'intellectuals' pretend that women have somehow always been 'oppressed' by men, that all men are 'rapists', that women must always be 'at war' with men, and most of all they insist that the disadvantages given to women by nature must somehow be redressed by the government.

If the two ladies in London and New York had lived 100 or even 50 years ago, there would have been no contradiction between their way of life and their 'feminist' views. But in view of the theses of feminism today, their position only makes people laugh.

The modern version of 'feminism' naturally ignores the fact that it was only at the beginning of this century that medical science managed to suppress child mortality. Prior to that women invariably had almost continual pregnancies, as more than half of all the children born would die, and people needed and wanted big families. As a result, women did not finish having and caring for children until well after the age of 40 - and feminine 'careers' could not even be considered. Another fact that feminists ignore is that until the end of the 19th century, very few people ever moved more than a few miles from where they were born, because transportation was slow, uncomfortable, and very dangerous. There was no commuting, no mobility of labour, and very few job opportunities. It is only within the last 100 years that transportation has become efficient and safe, and it is that transportation that makes jobs for women possible.

The extremism of the 'new' feminists (and the naiveté of the general public) is best shown by their aggressive attitudes towards the acceptance of women into the army and the police. It is very difficult for any rational person to understand the general acceptance of women into these bodies. The obvious point of the police and the army is to protect people in case of danger, and for that purpose only the strongest, toughest and bravest people are required. Does anyone really believe that women are physically stronger, physically tougher and physically braver than men? Whom would one want to protect one in a dangerous emergency - Mike Tyson or a strong woman?

There was a good example of the effectiveness of women policemen some years ago in New York. Policemen there patrol in pairs, and in this case a man and a woman patrolman were paired together, and were pursuing a criminal known to be dangerous. At a certain point they parted company and proceeded in different directions, in order to try and encircle the fugitive. The male policeman had no luck in his direction, so he returned to the rendezvous where he had left his female partner. He found her sobbing hysterically, because she had just been raped by the criminal (who had succeeded in finding her), and then been chained up with her own handcuffs. Needless to say this bit of news did not strike terror into the hearts of the criminals in the South Bronx, nor did it reassure the New York public towards their police force. Although the incident was reported, it did not receive the publicity it deserved. Leaving aside the question of emotional make-up, it is obvious that the claims made that women are physically strong enough to serve in the army and the police are not based on reality, and that in order to be able to induct women, both services have been forced to drastically reduce the level of their physical qualifications and tests. The result is physically inferior policemen and soldiers.

The hypocrisy of the 'new feminists' was made very clear several years ago, when the largest feminist organisation in America (the National Organisation of Women) admitted that most of its members were lesbians, and announced that they were de-emphasizing 'feminist' causes in order to focus on 'lesbian' ones. Surprisingly, this piece of news did not receive the publicity that it merited, either.

Can we make a date for rape?

One of the most controversial and widely discussed topics in the United States in the last few years has been 'date rape', and like almost everything American it has been imported to England. What is interesting is that all the controversy has taken place about something that does not actually exist. The word 'date rape' is of course a propaganda word, and like all propaganda words it has no actual meaning - it is only intended to persuade the hearer of a particular point of view. In this case, the desired point of view is that the rules for rape on a date should be different to the rules for rape in other situations. Of course, such an idea is opposed both to law and to reason, which is why it is never said openly. Nevertheless, special rules for rape on dates are now applied at colleges and universities both in America and in England.

A case that arose recently at London University brought this point out very clearly. The circumstances were straightforward. A young man and a young lady who were friends but had never been lovers, went to a pub on a Friday evening. They had several drinks, and during the course of the evening, the young lady proceeded to get drunk, and began wandering around the pub kissing all the men in the room. Only with some difficulty was the young man eventually able to lead her out of the pub, and to take her home, but when they arrived at her lodgings, she insisted that he came in. Eventually he agreed. Once inside, she made repeated sexual advances. Now a gentleman might not have taken advantage of the lady's inebriated condition, but since the advent of feminism, there do not seem to be as many gentleman around as there used to be. In any case, this young man finally stopped resisting her and they went to bed. The next day when the young lady had sobered up, she regretted what she had done, and after several days she decided to go to the college and complain that she had been 'raped'. This was clearly outrageous. As Martin Amis said, 'I accept a woman's right to change her mind before, or even during - but not after.' Nevertheless, upon receipt of the young lady's complaint, the college asked the young man to appear before a committee to investigate the charges, and the young man was put under great pressure to plead guilty to a lesser offence, to apologise to the young lady, and to leave London to study elsewhere.

However, this young man was more clever and more courageous than most, and he went instead to the police, told them that he had been accused of rape and gave himself up. This meant that he had to be charged and tried in court, and the college investigation had to be cancelled.

Naturally this did not suit the college at all. They did not want the case to be heard in a court of law - they wanted to decide it by themselves according to their own rules. It suited the young lady even less - the last thing she wanted to do was to testify in an open court. Nevertheless, there was nothing they could now do. When the case came up in due course, the young man was acquitted, while the young lady was made to look completely ridiculous, and to receive a severe tongue lashing from the judge.

This young man was fortunate to escape; others have not been so fortunate. The problem is that most people today have forgotten what rape is, i.e. a very serious and violent crime, which society has always punished most severely. Indeed, apart from murder, it was the last crime to retain the sanction of the death penalty. It has nothing whatsoever to do with ungentlemanly behaviour. Indeed, if ungentlemanly behaviour had always been punishable by death, there might not be very many men left.

As for the inevitable tussling that has always gone on between men and women, and has always been a part of the ritual of courtship, to suggest that this has the slightest connection with the violent crime of rape is quite simply absurd.

Men and Women

One often hears discussion about the subject of women's 'equality' with men. Such discussions are both futile and harmful. It is rather like asking if a dog and a cat are 'equal'. Obviously they are neither equal nor unequal - they are simply different. They are both animals, but they are different species of animals. Man and women are both human beings, but they are different species of human beings.

Fortunately their differences are complementary. Indeed, that was clearly Nature's intention. Men are aggressive, women are conciliatory; men have a lot of ego, women have much less; women provide the compassion that men lack, as well as the refinement, the charm and the gaiety; men provide the solidity and strength that women need. In short, the differences between men and women are extremely important and very necessary for harmonious life.

Women's minds work very differently to men's. IQ tests have shown that the average IQ of a man and a woman is exactly the same. Nevertheless there are important differences both in the distribution of their IQs, and also in their specific abilities. Women's IQs tend to be grouped closer to the average, while men's tend to vary much more widely. In other words, idiots and geniuses tend to be men. Men and women also vary in different skills. For example, in tests involving words, women usually do better, while in tests involving spatial relationships women do not do very well. That is perhaps why there are very few women engineers (not, as feminists would pretend, because they have not been allowed to be engineers). It also perhaps explains why there have been so few good women artists. Drawing and painting is one thing that women have been encouraged to do since time immemorial, and there have been thousands of female artists - yet there is not one woman artist in the first rank, and only a few in the second rank.

Another difference between the sexes is that women have the ability to do several things at the same time. A woman can be sitting reading an important letter, be keeping an eye on her small son who is trying to set fire to the house, be watching the clock to see when the lunch in the oven will be ready, be listening for the doorbell because she is expecting the plumber, and be making amusing conversation with someone at the same time. Men can only do one thing at a time. But because of that they have stronger powers of concentration than women. An interesting example is bridge. More women than men play bridge, and among players of average ability, women players tend to play more reliably than men. Nevertheless at the highest level, only a handful of women have been good enough to play with the very top men. One of that handful, Dorothy Hayden, who won a World Championship for the USA, was asked why. She had no hesitation in saying that the reason was that men had a higher level of concentration. Women's ability to think about several things at the same time, although vital in their daily lives, and particularly with children, makes it more difficult for them to maintain the same level of concentration as men can on a single thing.

Another difference is that women's minds work much more quickly than men's, and they reach conclusions much faster. By contrast, men's minds work more slowly. And, of course, women are far more intuitive, and perceptive about people, generally. They also tend to have rather lower opinions of other women than men have of other men. In other words, women are more realistic, men are more generous.

Men and women are also very different in regards to sexual matters. Men are more interested in sexual excitement, women in emotional security. That is perhaps why women resent men's absences so much. The reason why a man has to go away is irrelevant to them - they simply do not like separations, because they consider them a threat. Also physical looks are also much more important to men than they are to women. That is not only because men and women have different sexual desires, but also because there is a wider range of qualities to which women are attracted.

The important point is firstly that men and women are very different and secondly that this is extremely desirable. Indeed this is what attracts men and women to each other. It is also the reason that the phrase 'double standard' is misguided and inapplicable when applied to men and women, because it carries the implication that men and women are interchangeable, and start from the same position in life, when it is clear that this is not the case.

"Going steady"

In the late 1950s *Life*, the American magazine, ran a big article on the 'love life' of pre-teens in America. Among others, the article featured a young girl from Kansas, aged 12, who had already 'gone steady' three times, and who was quoted as saying that she did not think that she would ever find 'true love'. Ridiculous as this may seem, the underlying philosophy of this phenomenon - namely that young people should take partners and 'go steady' with them as soon as possible - has not only permeated the United States, but has now spread to Europe. The reason for its pervasiveness in modern life here is, of course, 'the Sexual Revolution'. If girls go to bed with a man very quickly, they feel more comfortable if they then stay with him rather than moving on immediately. Such behaviour is also more acceptable to their parents, who prefer their daughters to be having sex with one young man, rather than with many. (Of course, the unspoken assumption is that there is no question of going out with young men without having sex.)

Naturally these developments have been welcomed by the young men - such arrangements are easier (one does not have to ring anyone up every evening), cheaper, (one does not have to spend as much money on a 'steady' as on a girl one is courting) and generally more convenient for them. Most of all they incur no responsibility. 'Going steady', or living with someone, carries no guarantee of marriage, or indeed of anything else.

The effect on the girls, however, is less agreeable. They are restricted to the small circle of their 'boyfriend's' menfriends, and they meet very few new young men. Those that they do meet are reluctant to approach them because they are already 'spoken for'. Furthermore, because almost all young people are now 'going steady', the girls become frightened of being on their own if they leave their 'boyfriend'. As a result, the attachments drag on long after all pleasure and feeling have gone. When they do finally terminate, the rupture carries the emotional trauma of a divorce, without having had any of the pleasures of marriage. In the process, the girls lose their youth, their morale, and often their looks.

Chapter Four

The U-Turn

Since the beginning of time, each generation has invariably done things differently from the preceding one. Each older generation has invariably grumbled about the way the following one was behaving, while each younger generation would invariably resent the interference of the older one. Naturally exactly the same thing goes on today, but this time there is a very significant difference. In the past, although every generation changed the details of life, no generation challenged the basic assumptions of the past. Today, it is the basic assumptions themselves that are being challenged.

The essence of civilisation is the refinement of things that are necessary for life into things that give aesthetic pleasure. Any roof and walls can protect us from the wind and rain, but civilised people want a house whose appearance both inside and out will give them continuous pleasure. (This, of course, has nothing to do with money - even the smallest flat or humblest cottage can be made cosy and comfortable.) It is necessary to eat in order to stay alive, but it is much more pleasurable to eat delicious food in an agreeable setting, and to combine eating with conversation and social intercourse. We have to wear clothes in order to keep warm but it has always been accepted that clothes should be attractive as possible.

Since the Renaissance, the level of civilisation in Europe has been steadily rising, and one of the basic assumptions of the past 500 years has been that it was vital that our level of civilisation continues to rise. Indeed, it is only civilisation and reason that separate us from the animals. In the period between the Wars, Western civilisation seemed to stay on a plateau, neither rising nor falling very much, but in the post-War period, and particularly in the last thirty years, our civilisation has drastically changed direction and has started moving steadily and rapidly downwards for the first time in many centuries. In short, it has made an enormous U-turn. The reasons for this is perhaps not difficult to understand. It is simply that many people today in the West, including most of those under the age of 40, no longer give the same importance of civilisation and refinement.

An obvious example is the question of attire. Since time immemorial, it has been accepted that attire was a mark of one's level of refinement, as well as a mark of one's rank. For that reason, everyone tried to be attired as well as possible when they appeared in public. This basic assumption is no longer accepted however by a large part of today's younger generations (or even by some of the older ones). They believe that being well-dressed is something that one does only for an important occasion, and that the rest of the time it does not matter what one looks like.

What seems to have been lost sight of is that in civilised societies clothes are worn not only to keep warm, but also in order to look as pleasing as possible *to other people*. Appearance has always been an important element of civilisation, and when people make no effort to present a pleasing appearance (or do their best to present a displeasing appearance), they are not only aesthetically objectionable, but they are in effect insulting others. It is a way of saying, 'I don't care about your sensibilities, and I am not going to make the slightest effort for you.' We bathe not only because it feels nice to bathe, but because if we did not bathe, then we would stink and offend others. It is this consideration for other people that civilisation is based on. The question of shaving is similar - men do it not only because it makes their face feel well, but also because a stubble of beard is repugnant to others. Thus, when a man does not bother to shave, it is an act of contempt for others, as well as being aesthetically displeasing.

Why has this phenomenon become so widespread? Why do so many people present an unpleasant, or even disgusting appearance? There seem to be several reasons. One is that in the Socialist atmosphere which prevails today, it is considered that there is something wrong with being well-dressed - 'if everyone cannot be well-dressed, then no-one should be well-dressed' is the line taken. Of course, being well-dressed or just presentably dressed, has nothing to do with money, but that point is always ignored. It is even considered 'unfair' to have good taste, if other people don't have any. A second factor is that a shoddy appearance gives people a silent way to give vent to feelings which would be shaming if spoken aloud. They can insult people without speaking a word. Finally, there is also the natural laziness of many people, which welcomes any excuse not to make an effort. (Indeed as few people have natural taste, once dress conventions have been abandoned most people no longer have any idea how to present a pleasing appearance.)

An even more important U-Turn is the modern attitude towards manners. Manners have always been considered the primary indication of one's refinement, and of one's acceptance into polite society. This assumption, too, is now challenged, and emphasis is put more on whether one is considered a 'nice person', than on one's behaviour. It does not matter if Joe puts his feet on the dining room table, or does not bathe, or spits on the floor, if he is considered to have a kind heart. And yet it is only manners - which are based on consideration for other people - which enable people to live together in polite society. Without them, people soon sink back towards the level of animal behaviour.

These differences in basic assumptions makes it much more difficult for the older and the younger generations to communicate, because they are in effect speaking in different languages. If, for example, a young mother allows the dust in her house to pile up because she cannot be bothered to sweep it out; or lets her children eat food with their hands; or lets them pee on the floor; or lets them speak with a Cockney accent, any meaningful communication between her and her mother or mother-in-law becomes very difficult. Both sides are frustrated, yet they are not fully aware how this frustration has come about.

What has persuaded the younger generation to reject assumptions which have been accepted for centuries?

Certainly not their parents. Has it happened naturally? Can it be a coincidence? Obviously not. And yet?

"Modern" Assumptions

One of the most significant features of modern life is how many non-traditional and even startling assumptions have filtered into the consciousness of people from traditional backgrounds, without their having even been aware of it.

I 'But if she is happy?'

At a dinner party in the shires recently, a friend was sitting next to a refined lady of respectable background. She began to discuss a mutual friend who had recently abandoned her husband and family in order to live with another woman. My friend ventured the opinion that, leaving aside all moral and religious considerations, such behaviour was incredibly selfish and undignified. In a surprised voice his neighbour responded, 'But if she is happy...?' The interesting thing about this response was that in those

five rather short words this lady was making two unspoken, but extraordinary, assumptions, which she obviously
presumed that everybody shared.

The first assumption implicit in those words was that
sex automatically means happiness ('sex is happiness and
happiness is sex'.) This is a peculiarly Anglo-Saxon
notion. The majority of the world thinks that sex is a jolly
good idea, but they do not pretend that it necessarily leads
to happiness, let alone pretend that it *is* happiness. The
second assumption that those few words encapsulated was
that one's own personal 'happiness' is more important
than any other consideration, indeed that it is the only
consideration. In short, honour, dignity, morality, consideration for the people one loves, etc. cannot stand in the
way of one's own personal 'happiness'. Such an assumption would have been anathema to most civilised people
only a relatively short time ago. And yet, these two quite
extreme assumptions were now so deeply embedded in
this lady's mind, that she took it for granted that they must
also be in everyone else's.

II 'We didn't want to lose our children'

One of the things that one hears (almost ad nauseum) in
England is the phrase, 'We didn't want to lose our children.' It is invariably used by parents as an excuse for having allowed their children to do something unwise, undignified or positively harmful.

This statement also has implicit in it two very surprising assumptions. The first is that parental/child relations
are a one-way street in which children are allowed to do
whatever they wish, but the trembling parents are in danger of being sacked if they put even one foot wrong. The
second assumption, implicit in the first, is that the chil-

dren have not the slightest bonds of love and affection to their parents, and will, therefore, push off the moment anything occurs which displeases them.

Nowhere is this point of view seen more clearly than in the question of where and how young people live after finishing their education. Traditionally children would live with their parents until they were financially able to begin a family of their own, and would thus continue to receive their parents' financial support in the meantime. There are many families, especially on the Continent, where this custom continues. A French friend, who lives in Paris, had three sons in their twenties all living with her. When she asked the eldest son, then aged 25, if he was considering moving to a flat of his own. He replied "Certainly not, I am perfectly comfortable here." The more modern American approach, is that children leave home as soon as they finish their education, make their own way in the world, and support themselves financially. In England, however, there seems to be a third point of view, namely that children should have immediate 'independence' from their parents, but that their parents should pay for this 'independence', usually by giving their children allowances or buying them a flat – a kind of 'subsidised independence'.

Often it is flats bought by the parents that enable young people to live together, when they would not have been able to do so otherwise. Thus is established the principle of the one-way street – the children are 'independent' and free to do whatever they like, while the parents are obliged to pay but are not allowed to interfere in the slightest way. It is difficult to understand how such an idea came into such general acceptance with the English middle and upper classes.

Parents who follow the principle of the 'one way street' are sometimes criticised by some more traditional parents for being 'wet' or 'spoiling' their children. I would suggest that the word 'spoiling' is quite inaccurate in this context. 'Spoiling' has always meant allowing one's children to break the rules of behaviour without being punished. But that, of course, presupposes that there are rules. The point today is that, for the majority of children, there are no rules. Children are allowed to decide for themselves what they will eat or not eat; what they will wear; where they will go to school; at what age they will take lovers, etc. This has nothing to do with traditional 'spoiling' - it is quite simply an abandonment of parental responsibility.

III 'Perversions of homosexuality'

One evening I was discussing with a friend the subject of homosexuality. She held the view, quite common today, that homosexuality is no different from any other form of sex, and is neither morally wrong nor repugnant in any way. I wondered if she would maintain that view if faced with realistic details of homosexual behaviour, and as I knew her well, I began to describe to her in graphic detail some very common homosexual practices. She became more and more horrified, and at a certain point she was not able to continue listening any longer, and had to exclaim, 'But these are perversions of homosexuality'!!! There was then a moment's pause while she realised what she had just said. When she did, even she had to laugh.

It is amazing how many people there are today, who actually believe that there can be a separation between homosexual practices that are 'acceptable' and homosexual practices that are not. Although they do not express this thought as amusingly as my friend did, nevertheless the thought is in their minds.

Maturity

One of the most ironic characteristics of today's younger generation is the fact that they sincerely believe that they are more mature than previous generations. Yet the truth is precisely the opposite. Why do they live under this illusion? Almost certainly because they have sex earlier than previous generations did, and they therefore assume that this experience automatically makes them mature. They do not grasp the fact that sex does not make anyone mature - sex is simply pleasure, like playing football or watching a film, and pleasure does not make anyone grow up. What makes people grow up is precisely the opposite - it is doing things that one does not want to do, but that one has to do.

A century ago almost all children finished school by the age of 13 (although at 13 they were much better educated than the 18-year-old school-leavers of today). By the age of 23, those young people had had 10 years of life - 10 years of work, and responsibilities - and most probably of marriage and children. Today most young people only come down from university at 23, and are only just beginning life (because, of course, school and university have nothing to do with life). In short, today's generation is at least 10 years behind the generations of 100 years ago in maturity.

Even compared with the generation of 30 years ago they are much less mature, particularly the girls. In those days most girls left school at 16 years old, and by the age of 23 they had had seven years' experience of life, of work, perhaps of living abroad, of responsibilities, of social experience, probably of marriage, and perhaps of children. (As someone from my generation said to me, 'From the age of 18, we were told that we might be sitting next to the Prime Minister at dinner the next evening, and that we would have to be able to talk to him.' How many 18-year-olds would be able to do that today?)

There is another significant change that has taken place which affects the maturity of the new generation. In the past, young people would receive a stream of advice from older people all of whom had much more experience of life than they did - their parents, their relations, their teachers, etc. The advice they received very often did not coincide with their own inclination, and they rarely followed it. Nevertheless they were at least aware that what they had been told was sensible, and as they grew older they drifted back towards this advice. Today the situation is reversed. Young people are assured from every side that they are mature and knowledgeable almost at birth, and their parents - especially in the Anglo-Saxon countries -

make very little effort to guide them. 'Let them get on with it', is one of the most common clichés used by parents today to camouflage (even from themselves) their abdication of all responsibility. Even less do other family relations intervene any longer. As for teachers, most of them have become so confused that they do not know what to think themselves, let alone what to say to their students.

Now all this does not mean that young people today do not receive any advice. Of course they do, the asking and receiving of advice being an integral part of human intercourse. The difference is that the advice now comes from sources that do not have either the experience, the judgement, or the good will to discern what is responsible behaviour and what is not. What are these new sources? Firstly, their friends, who of course know no more than they do; then television and films; and finally, the examples that they see of how older people are behaving (which these days is usually very badly). None of this is helpful, and such sources only produce whatever clichés are currently in vogue - clichés that are not only frequently idiotic, but also very often destructive. When, therefore, things go badly for them, as they often do, young people have nothing to fall back on or return to, and are even more at sea than they were before.

Being prepared to listen to advice has always been considered an important sign of maturity. Of course, listening does not necessarily mean that the advice will be taken, but it does indicate a desire to learn about life and about the world, and it is also an admission that one does not yet know everything, which is the first ingredient of maturity. It is one thing to be aware of what is sensible and responsible, yet to choose for the moment to live one's life differently - it is quite another thing to behave irresponsibly, because one has no idea of how one should behave.

This illusion of their maturity is one of the many fantasies of today's younger generation, and it is a very dangerous fantasy, because on the one hand it makes them over-confident and opinionated, while on the other it keeps them ignorant and unable to cope with life.

"Lower" Education

One of the most pervasive fantasies of our times is the now widespread belief that academic results have a close connection with commercial or career success. This belief is now almost universal, despite the fact that the evidence is all to the contrary. Countless people who have not even finished school - let alone gone to university - have made fortunes starting from nothing, while the number of people who have failed to succeed in either business or the professions after a brilliant academic career is legion. Of those who do succeed in careers, very few are the ones for whom brilliant futures were predicted at school. Why then has this fantasy taken root, and why does it continue to be held?

Before World War II, relatively few people went to university, and of those that did, many did not pursue any career afterwards. Attending university is often described as 'higher education', and this is precisely what it is meant to be. It is education that is not necessary for life - school is meant to provide that - but it is education which enhances life, and makes it more pleasurable and fulfilling. Apart from a few special subjects like the sciences, medicine, and the law, university education has very little to do with preparing for a career, and indeed before the War employers were not particularly interested in whether job applicants had been to university or what their results there had been. (Ironically the one activity for which higher education is vital is working in government. One can make a million pounds without any education, but one cannot govern other people without a very good education.)

After the War, the educational situation slowly began to change as more and more people began going to university, and it changed dramatically in the 1960s when Macmillan's government 'opened up' education, and the number of university students skyrocketed. Faced with an avalanche of university degrees, employers naturally began to take them into account. As anyone who has had to do it well knows, choosing between job applicants is not easy. By using university degrees as a criterion, the choice became easier (although not necessarily any better). As a result, we have now reached a point when every young person desperately wants a university degree - not because they have any particular interest in the subject or in being educated at all, but simply in order to obtain a good job. In other words, university degrees are today regarded simply as passports to good jobs.

Unfortunately, university graduates are often disappointed. There was an example in the press recently about a young lady who had attended Oxford Polytechnic, and had come to London after graduation expecting to find a job, but was unable to do so. In a newspaper interview some years later, she described her feelings at that time as having been, 'Hey, I have a 2.1 from a university. Why don't you employ me?' Leaving aside the fact that a 2.1 from Oxford Polytechnic is not likely to impress very many people, the important point is that she felt that her university degree automatically entitled her to a good job.

The problem is that education and intelligence are not commodities that can be stocked on shelves, and handed out by the government to whomever wants them. The number of people who are intelligent enough for higher education is limited, and the number of people who can teach them is even more limited. On the one hand we have an avalanche of students desiring university degrees, while on the other hand there are only limited facilities to accommodate them. The government have dealt with this problem by taking the line of least resistance. They have turned the polytechnics - which originally were only vocational schools - into 'universities' simply by waving a magic wand and calling them 'universities', while they have encouraged the established universities to lower their educational standards so drastically that everyone who wishes to have a university degree can now be accommodated, regardless of talent, ability or intelligence. Of course, such degrees do not mean very much, and foreigners are well aware of the trivialisation of English 'university' degrees. Most university students in England today are not only wasting a lot of time, but also an enormous amount of other people's money.

Chapter Five

Does Two plus Two still equal Four?

A fundamental change which has gradually taken place within the last two generations has been the gradual disappearance of logic from supposedly serious discussion. I am not, of course, referring to private relations between people, where logic has always been subservient to the irrationalities of human nature. But until recently it had always been accepted that in general public discussion, (i.e. government, education, the legal system, etc.) anything that did not stand up to logic was not acceptable, and could not prevail. This point of view now seems to have been almost abandoned, to the point where it is very difficult to find today any supposedly serious assertions that stand up to serious analysis.

According to the dictionary, logic is simply the science and art of reasoning - and a logical person is one who is skilled in reasoning. Logic is usually expressed in premises leading to conclusions that abstract from their context the real reasoning that an argument embodies. These are often expressed in the following form:

A

Major premise:	All women are charming
Minor premise:	Frances is a woman
Therefore:	Frances is charming

or

B

Major premise:	All women are charming
Minor premise:	Frances is charming
Therefore:	Frances is a woman

Almost everyone would understand that the conclusion A is irrefutable, but that B is false. But as premises become more complicated, and become concealed in modern jargon (particularly when relating to emotional issues), it becomes more and more difficult for an average person, who has had no training in logic, to grasp what is really being said. In order for any conclusion to be true, it is necessary that the premises be both correct, and relevant. If either of the premises is faulty, the conclusion cannot stand, while if either of the premises is irrelevant (e.g. in the examples above, if the Minor Premise were, 'Frances wears brown shoes'), no conclusion can be drawn from them.

An example from a subject often debated may make this clear. Whenever the question of the death penalty comes up, the arguments usually run as follows: Those who are in favour of the death penalty begin (or jolly well should begin) by pointing out that the number of all homicides since the abolition of the death penalty since 1965 have more than doubled, while the number of murders have quadrupled. While not completely definitive in itself, this is a powerful fact to which opponents of the death penalty must reply. They inevitably reply by pointing out that over the same period all crime has increased dramatically. They then lean back and think that they have said something both logical and convincing. In fact, although it is quite true that all crime has increased over the last 30 years, what they are actually doing is replying to a fact (murders have quadruplrd) with a theory - namely, the assumption that the incidence of crime always remains the same for all crimes.

This would be expressed in logical terms, as follows;

Major premise: All crime has increased
Minor premise: Murder is a crime
Conclusions: The number of murders must increase proportionally

This theory contains two unspoken and unproven assumptions. The first is that all crimes in society increase or decrease at the same rate, regardless of other factors. This is demonstrably incorrect. Statistics clearly show that the incidence of crimes varies considerably, as between one crime and another, over different periods in time. Some crimes are fashionable in one era, others in another.

The second assumption is that all the penalties for crimes are continually changing, these changes do not affect the incidence of crimes (this in fact actually begs the question at issue). Suppose for example that in 1965, instead of abolishing the death penalty, the government had chosen to maintain it, but had instead decided to drastically reduce penalties for all other crimes. Obviously the incidence of other crimes would have increased considerably over the past 30 years, but there is not the slightest reason to think that the incidence of murder would have increased. Thus we see that the argument invariably put forward by opponents of the death penalty is a kind of sandwich - one fact is sandwiched between two fallacious theories, but presented as one supposedly logical argument.

There is a recent law case in America, that has now risen to the U.S. Supreme Court, which almost defies imagination. Some years ago, it came to the attention of U.S. Federal lawmakers that the drug, 'crack' (a derivative of cocaine) was quickly becoming the most popular and also the most dangerous drug in urban centres in the U.S. Accordingly the Federal penalties on 'crack' dealers were considerably stiffened, while the law enforcement agencies were urged to focus on the 'crack' trade. They did so, and as a result the number of Federal prosecutions and convictions for 'crack' dealing increased dramatically.

A problem soon surfaced, however. Almost all of the defendants in Federal prosecutions for 'crack' turned out to be black. This inspired the Los Angeles County Public Defender's Office to allege that Federal prosecutors were 'discriminating' against blacks, and this startling proposition was immediately taken up by academics, politicians and the press all over the country. Now if this argument were put into logical form, it would look as follows:

Major premise:	=	Only 13% of the U.S. population are blacks
Minor premise:	=	Over 90% of 'crack' defendants are blacks
Therefore:	=	Federal prosecutors are discriminating

Now even a child can see that this conclusion is palpably absurd. There is no form of human activity where all races are represented equally. In the particular case of drugs, each drug has its own 'market'. In the U.S. 'crack' is the drug favoured in low-income, minority neighbourhoods, because it is cheaper and acts more quickly. Hispanics favour powder cocaine, Asians favour heroin, and almost all defendants in LSD and marijuana cases are whites. Nevertheless, a U.S. District Judge, a Hispanic lady obviously not acquainted with either logic or the law, dismissed the government's case (U.S. *vs.* Armstrong) on the grounds that Federal prosecutors had the burden of 'proving' that they were not discriminating. The case is now pending before the U.S. Supreme Court, and there is no certainty what the Court's decision will be, because even in the Supreme Court there is no longer any certainty that logic will prevail.

What has caused this abandonment of logic? One reason perhaps is that logic is no longer taught in the educational system. Although I am not a Catholic, it happened that many years ago I attended a Catholic school. There was nothing particularly special about the school, nor was it reserved for brilliant pupils. It was simply a normal Catholic school of that time, run by Jesuits. Yet all of us were obliged to have studied logic by the age of 16. As a result, when we left school we had all had considerable exposure to logical reasoning. How many schools in England or America teach logic today? Indeed, it is very difficult for most people to even express what logic is.

Perhaps the most important reason that logic is out of favour today is because it is the ultimate intellectual discipline, and discipline of any sort is no longer fashionable in the Western world. What seems to be more fashionable is self-indulgence, and in particularly emotional self-indulgence. To anyone who wishes to indulge his emotions, logic is of course anathema.

A Hanging Offence

The subject of the death penalty returns to the news every few years, whenever there is another free vote in the House of Commons on whether to reinstate it. Invariably the House votes against reinstatement, although it is generally conceded that a large majority of the country is in favour of it. It is a subject which raises considerable emotive feeling, and yet very few people seem to be familiar with the facts.

Before the death penalty was abolished in 1965, considerable research was done by the government in the course of which many convicted murderers were interviewed. The conclusion reached by the psychologists involved was that the death penalty had not been a deterrent to those who had been interviewed. Now it seems very odd that the Government would have spent so much money and time on establishing something which is patently obvious. Clearly, the death penalty was not a deterrent to those interviewed - otherwise they obviously would not have committed murder. But it seems that the government 'experts' had never come into contact with logic, because they then jumped to the unwarranted conclusion that, as the death penalty had not been a deterrent to the people that had been interviewed, it was therefore not a deterrent to anyone. This was a good example of the Alice in Wonderland thinking which seems to prevail in our era, thinking that is contrary to all logic and to all experience.

If one looks back in history, there are two facts about crime which are perfectly clear. The first is that the more severe the punishment has been, the fewer crimes have been committed, which continues to be true today. The countries with the most severe penalties have the lowest crime rates - Singapore, for example. The second fact, however, is that regardless of the severity of the penalties, there are always some people who are prepared to commit criminal actions. In other words, although 99.9% of the population may be terrified by the death penalty, there is always a 0.1% that is not. Now it is perfectly clear that laws must be based on general human nature and experience, and not on the reactions of a few hardened criminals and/or psychopaths. Yet that is precisely what the government has done. Since the abolition of the death penalty in 1965, the number of all homicides has risen from less than 270 to almost 700 per year, and the number of murders has quadrupled. That means that since 1965 hundreds, and perhaps thousands of people have died, who might not have died. Are their lives less important than those of the murderers?

Apart from the question of deterrence, there are other arguments that are strongly in favour of reinstating the death penalty. An important one is that if justice is not seen to be done, ordinary people become dissatisfied with the conditions of law and order, lose respect both for the police and for the legal system and all crime increases. The result invariably is that law and order eventually begin to unravel altogether, which indeed is what is happening today.

The strongest argument, however, is the one that receives the least publicity. Thousands of years of experience has shown that (fortunately for all of us) the vast majority of mankind is incapable of taking another human life in cold blood. In the days when the FBI was the most efficient and respected law enforcement agency in the world, there were frequent occasions when they would corner a dangerous criminal in a house or refuge of some sort. At that point the script would often follow the movies. An FBI man would call on a loud speaker, 'Come on out with your hands up Joe, we have you surrounded.' Sometimes 'Joe' would indeed come out with his hands up, in which case there was no further story. But other times 'Joe' would shout back in time honoured movie fashion, 'Come and get me coppers.' Now at that point something would happen that never happened in the movies - Washington would be called and a special man would be flown out to the location for the specific purpose of going in to get 'Joe'. The man that Washington sent was neither particularly big, strong or young. He was invariably a man of average size, age and appearance. But that man had a rare quality that the agents surrounding the house did not have - he was prepared to to into that house and to kill a man in cold blood. The other FBI agents were not, even with the law behind them.

The obvious danger, once a man has killed and thus shown that he is capable of killing, is that he will kill again. In order to protect society, it is obvious that he must be prevented from doing so. This has always been the strongest reason for the death penalty. Apart from life imprisonment without parole, the death penalty is the only way to protect society from those who menace it.

Now if the debate were between the death penalty and imprisonment for life, the argument would be a very different one. But that is not the choice that we are faced with because, although all murderers are sentenced to life imprisonment, they are invariably paroled within 10-15 years. In other words, the choice we are now given is to either execute them or let them return to society. Now as most murders are committed by young men, that invariably means that convicted murderers are let loose on society at an age when they continue to be very dangerous. Those convicted after the abolition of the death penalty in 1965, began to be released in the 1980's in an ever-increasing stream into an unsuspecting society. Thus far previously convicted murderers who have been paroled are *known* to have claimed almost 100 lives after being released from prison. Now as only a small fraction of murders (and indeed of all crimes) are ever solved, this means that hundreds of people have died as a result of convicted murderers being released from prison. Yet the lives of these victims do not seem to be of the same importance in our society as the lives of the murderers.

As for those who insist that the death penalty is barbaric and uncivilised, they should perhaps consider that it has been the standard punishment for murder since time immemorial, not only in England, but in every civilised country in the world. Was the whole world barbaric and uncivilised before 1965?

Discrimination - Public or Private?

When I was young, my family lived in America, and we frequently went to Florida to visit my uncles. I still remember how shocked I was whenever I boarded a bus in Florida. Towards the rear of each bus there was a yellow line drawn on the floor, and all the black people in the bus were required to stand behind that line.

The public discrimination that existed in the American South has now disappeared, but America has now gone to the opposite extreme and is trying to prohibit private discrimination. This would necessarily destroy all individual freedom because private discrimination is what life is all about. When one chooses a school, when one chooses a job, when one chooses a house, when one chooses one's friends and when one chooses a wife or husband, one is obviously discriminating. (A girl who has six suitors and chooses to marry only one, is obviously discriminating against the others. Yet they have no right of complaint.) Indeed, it is the word 'discriminating' that has always had a good connotation, while it is the word 'indiscriminate' which has always had a pejorative one.

It is difficult to see by what right any government can interfere with personal choice - indeed just as no government should ever allow public discrimination, so no government should try to interfere with private choice. Yet this distinction does not seem to have yet permeated the American consciousness. Even worse, it has slowly been seeping into Europe, where it is now causing similar confusion.

Hypocrisy

Everyone knows that we live in an age of hypocrisy. There is nothing new about that - hypocrisy has been with us since the beginning of time. What is new is that the nature of this hypocrisy has altered. The dictionary tells us that hypocrisy is 'sham or pretence'. In the past such sham or pretence was usually used in support of the institutions of society - the Church, the Army, the State, the aristocracy, society, the family, etc. All these institutions have decreased drastically in importance over the last thirty or forty years, and yet the flow of hypocrisy continues unabated - indeed it is greater than ever. The reason is that hypocrisy has simply changed direction, and the hypocrisy that one hears today is much less about institutions, and much more about people. It invariably has to do with individuals trying to justify themselves, even if they have to insult other people's intelligence to do so. Whether it is a cabinet minister refusing to resign after a blunder (refusing even to admit that he has made a blunder); or a girl who batters her mother to death with a hammer and blames it on premenstrual tension; or a law school which awards a graduation degree to a girl who has been caught cheating, while at the same time announcing that, "No one can come to our school, and get away with cheating." At every level of society, the level of hypocrisy today has become shameless.

Another aspect of today's atmosphere is that, where in the past hypocrisy was invariably laughed at (sometimes even by those who were putting it forward), there is very little ridicule of even of the most shameless hypocrisy. Outrageous justifications are taken quite seriously, and even given importance in the press. It is one of the facts of life today that almost all levels of competence have been lowered. From cabinet ministers to street-sweepers, it has become very difficult to find people any longer who know how to do their job properly. This incompetence is inexorably intertwined with the general hypocrisy - instead of having to admit that they have simply been incompetent, everyone now pretends that it was someone else's fault. As they are not laughed at, they continue to do so again and again. Eventually the idea of responsibility for one's actions disappears.

The sphere in which this hypocrisy is most actively used today is, of course, politics. That too is not new, but what perhaps is new is its extent. One of the most striking examples of this is the government's attitude towards AIDS. In order to see the matter in perspective, the point that must be grasped is that very, very few people have actually died of AIDS. Indeed, the number of deaths from

AIDS in the Western World is derisory compared to any of the major illnesses. And yet the amount of money being spent on AIDS research in the Western World is many times what is being spent on any other disease. In short the fight against AIDS is regarded as something sacred, a holy crusade. The second fact to grasp is that not only has there never been any evidence that AIDS can be passed by normal sexual intercourse, but that all the evidence and the statistics indicate that exactly the opposite is true - namely that the risk of catching AIDS in normal sexual intercourse is about the same as getting hit by lightning. (Those who would like to pretend that there is a hetero-sexual risk from AIDS invariably refer to Africa, where heterosexual deaths from AIDS have been reported. What these people do not seem to be aware of, or perhaps do not wish to know, is that in Africa medical facilities are extremely primitive - needles are not sterilised, blood samples are not screened, etc. - and that therefore anyone who wanders into an African hospital has a very good chance of getting AIDS. Furthermore, the methods of diagnosing AIDS in Africa are primitive and extremely unreliable. Finally, the amount of funding in Africa to deal with AIDS is astronomic compared to other diseases. For example in 1992-93 the World Health Organisation supplied $6 million to Uganda to fight AIDS, and $57,000 for all other diseases. It is hardly surprising that the number of Aids cases in Africa is wildly exaggerated.

The greatest heresy of all is the belief that AIDS is caused by the HIV virus. And yet, although many people who die of AIDS are also infected with HIV, no one has ever found the slightest evidence that HIV causes AIDS. Indeed the evidence is all to the contrary, and even Dr Luc Montagnier of the Pasteur Institute, the French scientist who first discovered the HIV virus, has publicly admitted that HIV cannot cause AIDS on its own. Yet when a distinguished doctor in California produced evidence indicating that HIV is not the cause of AIDS, his grants were cut off by the U.S. government.

Why do we have to struggle with all these myths when they are plainly not true? The answer is, as always, political, and in this case malevolent. If AIDS comes from the HIV virus, then it is like catching a cold, and therefore no one's fault. But if AIDS is in fact a result of homosexual practices (or, what is even worse, a result of the drugs taken to facilitate these practices) as all the evidence suggests, then those who catch AIDS have only themselves to blame. Such an admission would be political anathema. Responsibility for one's own actions is not in fashion today. And if the group concerned are homosexuals, it would rock the very foundations of all 'politically correct' thought. In short, the truth is not acceptable, if it is 'politically incorrect'.

Both in this country, and in the United States, millions of pounds have been spent in advertising about AIDS, and promoting the myth that heterosexuals are at risk. Why should our own governments lie to us and waste so much money? Well, firstly, we have to face the fact that our governments lie to us quite regularly. Secondly, we must understand that our governments want people to donate money for AIDS research, and they know very well that no-one is going to do that, if they believe that the only people affected by AIDS are homosexuals and drug addicts. Finally, and worst of all, for political reasons our governments do not wish homosexuals to be embarrassed or humiliated in any way, or to feel that they are the only ones being singled out by this disease. So they have no compunction about spending vast amounts of money, or affirming propositions which are completely untrue. (In this connection, it is interesting to note that the general belief that AIDS is caused by the HIV virus did not come from any serious or distinguished scientific forum, but was the result of a statement disseminated by the US government at a press conference in 1984. Such an occurrence is, of course, unprecedented in medical history, and makes the political nature of the government's response very plain.)

One of the reasons that Socialism is fallacious is that its theories takes no account of human weakness or folly, and invariably assume that anyone who finds himself in a disagreeable position must be there because of the fault of others. In short, they deny that there is any such thing as personal responsibility. As it is only human nature to try to avoid fault or responsibility if one can, it is not very difficult to persuade people that nothing is ever their own fault. Nor is it surprising that the bubble of hypocrisy in the modern world is getting bigger and bigger. What is regrettable is that more people do not take the trouble of pricking it with ridicule. That is the one thing against which hypocrisy cannot stand.

Indian Cows
and such

If one had to choose the single most important principle in life, it would perhaps be that one must always accept the consequences of one's own actions. This has been true since time immemorial. Yet, today, this principle is no longer fashionable, and people are led to believe not only that they can have it both ways in life, but even that they deserve to have it both ways.

The independence achieved by so many new nations over the last 50 years highlights this problem. The colonial rule that preceded independence was stable and reasonably prosperous, but it was perfectly understandable that the people under colonial rule wished to have their independence. If one had been in their place, one would no doubt have wished for the same thing. The problem is that having obtained their independence, they were not prepared to accept its consequences - namely, the corruption, the inefficiency, the atrocities and the brutality (all on a scale that cannot even be imagined in the West), which are endemic in less civilised and less developed countries, and particularly in countries with no traditions of freedom or democracy. The result has been that since independence, standards of living in these countries have fallen alarmingly, law and order has collapsed, and atrocities take place almost continuously. Almost all of these countries have, therefore, repeatedly appealed to the West for money and aid, and have received it. Nevertheless many of them have suggested that the West is somehow to blame for their present predicament.

A graphic illustration of the problem is India, a subcontinent that was broken up into at first two, and later three, separate countries. By contrast to other colonial nations, the Indians have a considerable history of civilisation and culture behind them, and it was perfectly natural for them to wish to be independent. Despite their higher level of culture and civilisation, however, what they did not have was any traditions of freedom or democracy, and they, too, have fallen prey to corruption, incompetence and brutality. Their independence did not begin auspiciously, as over three million people were killed in religious riots and fighting within the first few days of independence, while still today incompetence and corruption reign supreme – indeed recently three governments fell in a period of two weeks.

It was not very long after Indian independence that food production began falling and from having been a food exporter in the past, India became a food importer, and even suffered widespread starvation. The West had to come to their assistance again and again. Nevertheless, the population continued to multiply, while food production kept falling. One of the most vivid pictures of India taken home by visitors in the 1960's and 1970's were the enormous piles of American aid grain sitting in Bombay rotting because the railway system was not able to take the grain inland where it was needed.

But perhaps the best symbol of independent India are the cows. The Hindu religion considers cows to be sacred, which means not only that they cannot be slaughtered and used for food (only the Moslems, who do eat meat, are allowed to slaughter only a specified small number of cows per year), but that no-one is allowed to touch them or interfere with them in any way. That means that cows in India wander wherever they like, eat as much as they like and cause as much damage to crops as they like. The last time that the Indian cow population was measured some years ago, it was estimated that there were over 400 million cows. Today, the number would probably be nearer to 500 million. It is difficult for the average person to grasp just how much 500 million cows eat in one year, or how much damage they cause. What is obvious is that without the cows the standard of living in India would be very different.

If the Hindus choose to regard the cow as sacred, they are obviously perfectly free to do so. But should the rest of us be asked to subsidise their religious views?

Single - or just Unmarried?

One of today's most controversial topics is the increasing number of 'single' mothers. According to DSS statistics, the number of people receiving One Parent Benefit, (which began only in 1977) has now passed 1.5 million. Of this 1.5 million people, over 500,000 are considered 'single' mothers (as opposed to widowed or divorced mothers).

There is something odd in these statistics. In the late 1950s the *New York Times* ran some articles on the New York public high school system, and one of the articles pointed out that at Benjamin Harrison High School (a school on the edge of Harlem), 25% of the senior class were pregnant. In view of the pill and the many other contraceptive devices that are available now, and were not available then, not to mention continuous government

advertising campaigns about 'safe sex', and school indoc-
trination about sex, it is difficult to believe that the frequency of unwanted pregnancy among young girls today
is anything like what it was 40 years ago. The question
remains, why has there been such an increase in 'single'
mothers?

I would suggest that the answer can only be a greater
frequency of 'wanted' pregnancies, rather than unwanted
ones. In this connection it is important to differentiate
between 'single mothers', and so called 'unmarried'
mothers - 'single' suggests that the mother has been left by
the father and lives alone, whereas 'unmarried' refers to a
mother who is living with a man, but is not married.

Some years ago a man came to the office where I was
working in order to apply for a job. When asked what his
previous employment had been, he said that he had been
working for the Department of Social Services, investigat-
ing people claiming benefits. In particular, he visited 'single' mothers to see whether they were actually living
alone. When asked what his experience had been, he
replied that in almost every case, there had been a man,
usually the father, living with her. The father would
arrange to be absent on the one day per month when the
social worker would visit, but would live with the woman
the rest of the time. When asked why he wished to change
his job, our applicant replied that he was too frightened to
continue, because he was daily being threatened with
bodily harm by the men living with these 'single' mothers
if he ever showed his face again.

It is not difficult to understand why this happens.
Even the most honest people in the world (people who
would not dream of stealing 10p) have no compunction in
stealing from the government. The rationale invariably is

'Everyone else is doing it', or 'After all, it's our money'. Some years ago I employed a secretary who professed extremely high principles, and who severely criticised anyone who fell short of her standards. In due course she married and became pregnant, and when the time for the baby was approaching, I asked if she intended to come back to work afterwards. She replied, 'I would not tell anyone else, but I trust you. I am not coming back to work, but I have to pretend that I am coming back in order to obtain the government benefits.' Even she had no hesitation in taking the government's money. Of course, what is never taken into account is that the government has no money of its own, and only has what it collects in taxes from its citizens - in other words it is other people's money that is being stolen.

If the government makes a rule that you have to be a 'single mother' in order to collect benefits, every mother will pretend to be 'single'. By the same token, if the government said only parents who lived together were to receive benefits, the same people would ensure that they qualified. It is simply the way of the world.

The Socialist

Garden

The greatest irony about the collapse of communism in Russia is that most people are now convinced that the threat of Communism in the world has receded, while in the West the Hard Left is becoming continually stronger and more powerful. Why does the Hard Left continue to thrive? After all, the aims of the Hard Left in the West are no different from the aims pursued in Soviet Russia or Communist China - the destruction of education, the dissolving of all spiritual or family ties, the elimination of the idea of personal responsibility for one's actions, total dependence on the State, the acceptance of envy as a respectable emotion, etc. None of these aims, is, of course, compatible with freedom, so in order for the Hard Left to succeed freedom must somehow be eliminated.

It is particularly interesting to think about why the

Hard Left continues to be so successful in England despite the fact that there has been a Conservative government for 17 years. Perhaps the single most effective reason for their success here has been their seizure of control of the educational system during the early 1960's. This was accomplished by a massive infiltration of the educational system, when it was expanded in the early 1960's, by people sympathetic to Hard Left views, and most decisively by their seizure of the reins of administration in the educational system, which enabled them to control the appointments and promotions within the teaching ranks, and thus to control both the teachers and the curriculum. In addition, through the medium of so called 'Teacher Training' colleges, they have been able to brain-wash all the new young teachers coming into the system, and to imbue them with Socialist dogma with antipathy to Western civilisation. The result is that there are very few people in this country, under the age of 40, who have not been influenced by Socialist 'teaching', regardless whether they are aware of it.

Another strong reason for its success is that the Hard Left continues to appeal to what is worst in human nature – to the side that is unfortunately present in some degree in all of us – and to justify the basest actions by appeals to emotions and by the rejection of truth and reason.

But perhaps the real reason that the Hard Left have succeeded so well is the extent of the naiveté in the Western world. Even today, very few people can bring themselves to believe that at bottom the Hard Left do not 'mean well' - they are still reluctant to accept that the Hard Left wishes to do harm, to destroy, and to extinguish Western society and Western civilisation. Even more decisive is the fact that of those who do understand, very few are prepared to fight back. That is the real strength of the Hard Left - human weakness. They have grasped the fact that human nature is such that ordinary people only want to get on with their own lives, and are rarely able to organise any resistance to any group that is organised, determined and completely ruthless, no matter how malevolent that group may be.